25 Ways to Prepare for Marriage

(Other than Dating)

Blessings on your journey!!

Jamal Miller

Jamal Miller

ISBN-13: 978-0692250716

ISBN-10: 0692250719

Dedication

To my Dad and Mom, Rome and Cynthia. You have been the most influential people in my life. You gave me a foundation upon which I have built my life. To you I credit the early years, which are the most crucial for any child. I love you more now than I ever have, and that love grows each day.

To my Apostle, Pastor, and Father in the Gospel, Dr. Matthew Stevenson. I thank you for seeing what God was doing in me at such a young age, and not only helping put a language to it, but also a body. I will never be able to repay you for what you have sacrificed in order to see me reach my full potential. All I can say is, "Thank You!"

To my wife. You are the fruit and reward from which this book is written. It is you who God used to make my dreams come true. Our Facebook Love Story has changed thousands of lives, and inspired men and women to wait on God for their spouse. We did not just wait, we prepared. Thank you for preparing yourself for me. This is just the beginning my love.

Table of Contents

Section 1

Section IV

Section V

Foreword

There are many books about dating and marriage. Jamal Miller writes this book in such a way that it clearly stands apart from the others because of his transparency. The major element separating this literary work from others is Jamal's willingness to be honest and open about his life, shortcomings, and successes.

Throughout this book you can expect to be challenged, encouraged, uplifted, and convicted. Jamal writes about his personal struggles with pornography, his successes in his relationship with his now-wife, and he imparts bursts of wisdom throughout the entire book. I especially love that Jamal chose to write this book as an action plan purposed to keep the reader engaged and motivated to maturing before and in a relationship. He chose to give the reader more than just information.

My wife and I chose to wait until our wedding day to kiss. Our entire courtship lasted one year and eight months. My wife and I are major supporters of choosing to honor God in relationships. I truly believe this book promotes the healthy and biblical practice of honoring God. I am also sure you will enjoy it—as have I.

I look forward to reading more of Jamal's literary works, and I pray you are encouraged by what he has written.

Cornelius Lindsey

Author of *So, You Want to be Married?*; *I'm Married. Now, What?*; *Not For Sale*; *So, You Want to be a Man?*; and *Learning How to Walk*

www.corneliuslindsey.com

A Note from my Wife

First off, I want to share with you how proud I am of my amazing husband. His commitment to God and our family is simply beautiful. When my husband began to write this book, I immediately began to think back to all of the conversations I had with friends and family while I was single. I then turned to the moments where Jamal and I were courting. The number one question I've been asked while being unmarried and married is, "How did you remain content during your time of waiting?" The root of my answer always stems from my personal relationship with Jesus Christ. I chose to fall in love with Him. I made him the center of my life. I desired to please him more than those who were around me; more than those who may have doubted his strength and power in me due to unbelief.

When you seek the face of God and let go of your agenda and embrace Him, your perspective has no choice but to change and submit to the word of God. Jamal does a great job, through his life, showing how to navigate through your single years to become confidently ready for marriage. In *25 Ways to Prepare for Marriage other than Dating*, my husband talks about pivotal preparation points that every man and woman should take heed of. I pray this book inspires you the same way my husband inspires me.

Introduction

My Story of Preparing for Marriage

God began to awaken my desire for marriage at the very young age of 12 years old. It did not make any sense at all, but I began to have dreams about having a family and loving my future wife. I took it as far as writing letters to my future wife. My parent's went through what most marriages encounter, but they endured each trial. They gave me the motivation to want to lead my future wife and children God's way. This was a good and a bad thing. When I entered into high school I still did not have a girlfriend, but I desired one very badly. I was shorter than most guys in my class, so I learned how to win girls over in other ways. I saw that most guys did not really know how to make a girl happy other than doing the bare minimum. I would find a girl who had a guy and be tempted by the challenge of stealing her away. This was a demonic setup to undermine what God was trying to do within me.

Many of you can relate to being awakened and wanting to "have someone" to call your own, even before you understood the significance and power of a covenant relationship. You entered into a relationship thinking it was the thing to do because everyone else was doing it. Your parents may have even thought it was "cute" for you to be crushing on the little boy in your class. Or, maybe your dad celebrated you when you brought multiple girls to the house. Whether you like it or not, the moment you began to open your heart up to intimate feelings towards someone you were preparing yourself for marriage.

My story continues when I became a member of a passionate youth ministry in my town during my junior year of high school. The youth pastor did not play any games when it came to living holy for God. He challenged me and a few other youth to commit to not dating our entire high school career. He taught us that our relationships with God were still being established and entering into an intimate relationship would interrupt the process of God becoming the lover of our soul. The first thought when this commitment was placed before us was, "If I can't date, then how am I going to prepare for marriage? This question took me on an8-year journey of God showing me there are many other ways to prepare for marriage other than dating. I went on to graduate from high school still never having a girlfriend nor involving myself in an intimate relationship with the opposite sex. I dedicated those 4 years to Jesus! I went on to college with so much more value on who I would open my heart up to for a relationship. My heart for you as you read each of these 25 ways is that you will discover who you are, lay a solid foundation for your future marriage, and fall in love with God's purpose for your life. This book is going to make your marriage dangerous (in a good way). Your future spouse is going to thank you for taking the time to invest in the thing that will change the course of your life.

Dating is not the only way to prepare for marriage and also can be very dangerous if not done God's way. In this book you are going to learn 25 ways to prepare for marriage. Each way is set to help you not only prepare for marriage, but also be a better follower of Christ. It is God's desire to transform you into the likeness of His Son.

Now, let's pray!

"Father, I ask you for grace upon each single person that is reading now. That they may continue to live a life laid down for you and your Kingdom. Give them faith for the future to know you have their life in the palm of your hand. I pray that Your Peace will guard their hearts and minds. Let them bear more fruit in this season than ever before. In Your name I ask these things. Amen!"

The Gift of Singleness

In order to apply the principles you will find in this book you must first have a proper perspective of the season you are in. If you are reading this book you are either unmarried, not in a relationship but desiring one; or unmarried, in a potential relationship hoping it develops into more. If you are in one of these two categories then having a biblical perspective of the season of singleness will help you to value this time even more. Let's dive into the word of God, and then you can have fun with the 25 different ways to prepare for marriage.

> "Now as a concession, not a command, I say this. I wish that all were as I myself am. But each has his own gift from God, one of one kind and one of another. "(1 Corinthians 7:6-8 ESV)

> I say this as a concession, not as a command. But I wish everyone were single, just as I am. But God gives to some the gift of marriage, and to others the gift of singleness. (1 Corinthians 7:6-8 NLT)

Now, I provided both translations because this is one passage of scripture that can be misunderstood very easily. In the New Testament the word gift simply means in the Greek, charisma or grace. When you view a gift in practical terms you see it is something someone has given you so it may be utilized as an opportunity.

Paul's sincere passion in writing this was to establish that regardless of whether you are married or single, it is an opportunity to serve God's kingdom. But, it would be easier to get some things done while unmarried. I was able to during my season of being single to accomplish and attain a lot. From my degree, moving to a new city, becoming an ordained pastor, and going on various mission trips. Those experiences and accomplishments all contributed to my future marriage. I thank God I viewed my unmarried season as an opportunity to prepare, grow, and establish myself for marriage. Our online community, Married and Young, was birthed out of the desire to see the marriage rate increase among bible believing Christians, so please know I am a huge advocate for people getting married. It is through Godly marriages that godly offspring come forth, communities are impacted, and worldviews are shifted. My prayer as you take each way to prepare for your future marriage is that it will deepen your understanding of why Christ must be the center of your season of preparation. Many today are attempting to work the invention without reading the "How to" Manual from the Inventor. God is the inventor of marriage, so it would be a great idea to understand it from His perspective.

After about six months of being married, I realized something that I pray every unmarried person meditates on. Every second I spent before I said I do, was preparation for marriage. All the things I accomplished, and all the things I failed to do all contributed to my present day marriage. Before I married my wife I was a huge proponent for preparing for marriage. Now that I am married, I cannot stress how important it is to prepare for the covenant that changes everything.

What this Book is not

1. This book is not a get married quick scheme.
   - It will not speed up the process for you finding your spouse.
   - It is not a way to impress God in order to get him to have your spouse knocking at your front door upon you reading the last sentence at the end of this book.
   - It is not the Bible that you must follow it to a tee in order to be fully prepared for marriage.

What this Book is

I purposely wrote this book as an action plan filled book. An action plan is a plan that propels you into forward motion. Each chapter was written with just enough information to put it into use. If you are reading this in order to know how to get your spouse to come quicker, then that is the wrong mentality. Your goal in reading this book should be to learn more about who God has created you to be, grow your roots deeper in Him, and prepare yourself for a covenant that changes everything. Each chapter will give you a glimpse into what will be challenged in marriage so you can better equip yourself for it.

There is no magic formula, but what I can say is this, by implementing the strategies in this book in your life, they will help you develop into a person ready for marriage.

Section 1

Chapter 1

Fall Madly in Love with Jesus

And he said to him, "You shall love the Lord your God with all your heart and with all your soul and with all your mind. This is the great and first commandment. (Matthew 22:37-38, ESV)

This is where my story begins. Before I fell in love with God, I viewed life through a foggy glass. After the love of Jesus invaded my heart everything became clear. That clarity was because I found the singular purpose of living; to Love God and make His love known. This revelation is the entry point into everything you are called to be. Outside of His love you find those who are unforgiving, unloving, slandering others and having no self-control (2 Timothy 3:3 NLT).

There is no love without a choice. Many ask why did God put the tree of knowledge of good and evil in the Garden of Eden if he knew Adam and Eve would be tempted to eat from it? If we were not given the ability to make decisions, we would not have the freedom to choose love. God did not make robots, for we are His creation, given free will. Our commitment to not only love Jesus, but also choose Him every day is the beginning of our learning how to commit in relationships. My relationship with Jesus taught me how to love my wife because I saw how he loved me. The more you cultivate and go deeper in your love for Christ before your spouse arrives on the scene, the easier it will be to choose and love your spouse unconditionally each day. This is the single most important decision you will ever make in your life. Having a burning relationship with God will protect you from falling for someone that is not suitable for your life.

While working for a startup company when I first moved to Chicago, there was a co-worker who was very attractive to me. I attended a Christian college right out of high school, so the majority of the girls I encountered were Christians. This co-worker was one of the first unbelievers I had an attraction to in that manner. The one thing that kept me from entertaining the thoughts of pursuing her was my discerning of her not being a lover of Jesus. My relationship with God is dependent upon my obedience to God's word. His Word plainly states in, 2 Corinthians 6:14, "Do not team up with who are unbelievers. How can righteousness and wickedness have in common?" It is very easy to fall into the trap of the enemy and cast your pearls before the swine. There is nothing Satan wants more than to have you marry someone who is not the will of God for your life.

What is a Lover of God?

When I encountered God for the first time in my bedroom at the age of sixteen, it set the course for the rest of my life. This defining experience was not based on how messed up I was, but how amazing He was. It was a combination of Isaiah's, "Woe to me!" I cried. "I am ruined! For I am a man of unclean lips, and I live among a people of unclean lips, and my eyes have seen the

King, the LORD Almighty, and David's, 'One thing I ask from the Lord, this only do I seek: that I may dwell in the hose of the Lord all the days of my life, to gaze on the beauty of the Lord and to seek Him in his temple.'" Both of these experiences illustrate what the beginning of becoming a lover of God looks like. First, recognizing how jacked up you are, but not stopping there, for it should make you fall madly in love with how amazing, perfect, majestic, and holy God is. Second, that love is even further demonstrated on His end because He chooses to love you unconditionally despite your filthiness. That's real love! **Let's pause now, and thank God for the simplicity of His love.**

> *Father, thank you for choosing to love me in the middle of my junk, and not allowing anything I have done to stop you pursuing me with reckless abandonment. It is for you that I live and breathe. Amen.*

Now, being a lover of God moves from us to the place where it is all about knowing Him. This serves as the key source of strength to loving Him no matter the cost. Mike Bickle, founder of the International House of Prayer, explains it well.

> *"First and most important, who is God? What is He like? What kind of personality does He have? Our ideas about God—who He is and what He is like—come naturally through our relationships with earthly authority figures. When these are distorted, so are our ideas about God.*

*I believe the greatest problem in the church is that
we have an entirely inadequate and distorted idea
of God's heart. We can experience short-term
renewal through prayer and ministry. But to
achieve long-term renewal and freedom, we must
change our ideas about who God is."*[1]

The journey of discovering God is a journey indeed. It is a journey you will be on for the rest of your life. He is and will always be your first love. Even as relationships develop and grow in your life, no relationship should ever overtake your relationship with God. I became so fascinated with God I began to ask questions that allowed me to see Him as a real compassionate person versus the "Big Guy" upstairs. These questions propelled me into His Word, which is the greatest asset to your discovery of God. Every day before I went to sleep I would say, "God, is there anything else I need to know before I go to bed?" When I would wake up each morning the first words out of my mouth were, "God, how was your night?" I was so consumed with the person of God.

Your language towards God reflects how you view Him. Is He Daddy God, or is He a distant unknown figure you have only heard about from others? Who is God to you? Do you run from Him when you mess up or do you run to Him? Is He more important to you than money, fame, or marriage? Does pleasing Him bring joy to your heart? In John 8:32, Jesus tells the crowd that we will know the truth, and the truth will set us free. The truth is God Himself in Christ Jesus. It is by knowing

---

[1] Mike Bickle, *Passion for Jesus*, (Lake Mary: Charisma House, 2007), 1.

God that you will unlock everything within yourself. For you no longer exist because according to Colossians 3:3. You have died, and your life is now hidden with Christ in God. There are many ways to grow in God, but rest in knowing it is He who sustains you, not how long you pray, or how much you memorize the bible, all of it is to discover Him, and make Him known.

Establish a consistent devotional life.

If you are a faithful follower of Christ and are submitted to a local church then this should not be a challenge. The truth is even the most committed lovers of Jesus have a hard time having a consistent devotional life. When you get married this will be one of the most attacked areas of your walk with God. You will be tempted due to the excitement of the new season of marriage to neglect your time with God. It is so dangerous to get into a relationship and not have this component nailed down. When you get the revelation that the person you are is because of Him, then you know your entire life is dependent upon a growing relationship with God. I am the man I am today because of the history I built with God during years of being single.

I remember a specific time I went on a personal fast to really draw close to Him. My goal was not to get anything from God. All I wanted was to hear His voice. I was sick of being selfish and self-centered, constantly coming to Him with questions and concerns about my timeline. During that fast I expected to grow in patience, but I became even more anxious. I felt like all the lights in the room were being pointed at me and all of my flaws, insecurities, and disqualifications were being put on display. What I did not know was the fast had activated

John 15:2 which says, "He cuts off every branch in me that bears no fruit, while every branch that does bear fruit He prunes so that it will be even more fruitful." You see, it is the desire of God to make you more like Him, but it does not always feel good. When I see myself getting mad easily, or frustrated with myself I know there is only one thing I need and that is His presence. Become a lover of His presence not when you need something from Him, but because you need Him.

Go on Personal Spiritual Retreats.

"Consecrate yourselves, for tomorrow the Lord will do wonders among you." (Joshua 3:5 ESV)

This verse brings so much excitement to my heart each time I read it. The biblical definition of consecrate is to "set apart." You agree that we all have good and bad seasons throughout the year, and as a result need to have times of refreshing where we rededicate our lives back to Christ. This is the power of spiritual retreats!

The first lesson I learned in marriage in regards to my relationship with God was my wife is the greatest threat to it. Let me explain. When I was single, I did not have someone waiting to spend quality time with me when I got home from work, so it was easy to retreat and have alone time with God. After getting married, everything changes. Bob Sorge, best-selling author of *The Secret Place*, teaches to have a yearly, blocked off weekend where you go away to be with God. This makes way for you to reignite your relationship with God, attain perspective for your current and upcoming season, and make intercession for those closest to you. My wife and I schedule time to go away with God for a period of refreshing with Him. Learn to do this now for it will be a blessing to you and your future spouse.

Learn Not to Worry, but Trust God

If you only knew how much time I took worrying how God was going to bring my spouse into my life. After graduating from college it was like okay, "God, I'm ready," a phrase I would repeat every day in my prayer time. Each minute I spent worrying how she was going to come, or when she was coming robbed me from enjoying the season God had me in. If you are single and waiting on God for your spouse, please do not waste time wondering how God is going to do it. Trust that He will do it. Your marriage season will come in God's timing.

Take faith risks for God to break fear and learn obedience.

Moving to Dallas, TX to attend college was one of the first major faith risks taken in obedience to God. Since that time I have done countless more things that only can be understood through the lenses of faith. I believe with all of my heart that each faith risk I took before I met Natasha helped me take the dive to tell her after meeting her face to face 9 hours earlier, "I'm all in". I had learned when something was and was not God due to my history with God. What history are you developing with God? What risks have you taken out of obedience to His voice? Fear will always be present when a great opportunity is standing in front of you, but He has not given us a spirit of fear! As I am writing the verse Hebrews 11:6 comes to mind, *"Without faith it is impossible to please God*". I begin to think back on the past few months and I could not recall something in my life that really took a lot of faith to believe for. With that being said, I said to God, "If your word says I cannot be pleasing to you without faith being involved, then God I give you full reign to STRETCH my faith. Do something in my life that will require me to place my full assurance and dependence upon you."

We can all relate to the moments while growing up when our parents yelled at us these phrases, "PUT THAT DOWN, GIVE ME THAT, or WHERE DID YOU FIND THAT?" and we always responded back with "WHY", then they respond with "BECAUSE THAT'S DANGEROUS YOU MIGHT HURT YOURSELF".

Praise God for parents that love us enough to protect us during our ignorant days from potential danger. There are many stories I can tell about dangerous things I did while I was a kid simply because I did not listen to my parents. We have learned from our parents that playing it safe in many situations will spare you your life. But, when gazing into Hebrews 11, I see a chapter of men and women who in no way played it safe. Actually, it was their lack of playing it safe that made them eligible for such a high honor.

We all desire to be pleasing to God. But, the reality is we cannot be pleasing without faith being involved. This is a simple reminder to throw off your safety goggles and stop playing it safe with God. I challenge you to pray one of the most dangerous prayers you can pray, "God stretch my faith." Trust me, HE WILL DO IT!

Chapter 2

Invest in Yourself

"Invest in yourself. It will pay you back for the rest of your life."-Anonymous

After four and a half hours of driving in a torrent rain storm from Monroe, Louisiana, I finally made it to Dallas, Texas. This would be the place I would spend the best, yet most challenging, years of my life—bible college. It was here that I gained friends from all around the world, was poured into by some of the greatest leaders in the body of Christ, and, most of all, learned how to value what God has invested in me. God has invested much in you, and it is your responsibility to respond by having those things cultivated.

Those who invest in themselves believe in the value they have to offer, but also recognize that others are dependent upon their success. Your future self and spouse will benefit greatly from your years of investing in yourself. I think back to the wise decisions and hard sacrifices I made in previous seasons from which I am now benefiting greatly. Live your life now with the confidence that you will be able to thank yourself later.

Go To School

Going to any type of post-secondary school whether it is college, technical college, or bible college not only helps you in the future, it will also provide a season in life where you can discover a lot about who you are. You can make many excuses as to why you can make it without going to school, but I promise you there are more reasons for why you should make the sacrifice and invest that time in formal training. Be wise when it comes to declaring your major. Many students today are selecting degrees that are not fit for His plan for their life. You should get a degree that is going to enhance what God has already invested in you.

Read lots of Books

I have always been an avid reader, but I also know many who have a hard time reading books. The reason you do not like to read is possibly because you have not figured out what you like. I like to read more than just to attain information. It is about exposing myself to new information. I love knowledge. While in college I had a pretty cool moment with God. In any given semester I had to read between 7-10 different books. I became frustrated with reading other peoples material and said to myself, "Man, I could be getting my own revelation and writing my own books while I'm wasting my time reading someone else's." The Holy Spirit quickly spoke up saying, "You have the ability to learn something in ten minutes that may have taken the author ten years to learn." That shut me up quick! Reading books is such an effective way to gain access to information more valuable than you could imagine depending on how well you apply it.

Start a Habit

Successful people do successful things, and those things are broken down into repeatable habits. What is something you aspire to do every day? When you do something for twenty-one (21) days straight then you are on the right path to making that activity a habit. Here is a list of things that can easily become a habit, eventually helping you become even more successful than you already are.

- Read a book a week.
- Connect with one person a week outside of your circle of influence.
- Workout.
- Share the gospel with a stranger. (the Cashier or a person in the line at the grocery store)
- Call a family member weekly to pray with them.
- Start a blog and post once a week.
- Take a class.

Chapter 3

Establish the Foundation of God's Purpose for Your Life

What you know about yourself determines what you give of yourself to others. By establishing the foundation of God's purpose for your life, you will have a guiding point for where He is taking you. Foundation is the key word here. God's purpose is not a destination, but a journey you will be on for the rest of your life. The foundation of that purpose is acknowledging God being pleased with your life as the focal point. When God spoke immediately after Christ being baptized by John in Matthew 3:16, God spoke, "This is my Son, whom I love; with Him I am well pleased." God was pleased with Christ before He died on the cross. God is not pleased when we do, but when we are. Obedience is the key. Your purpose will ignite when you establish it upon being pleasing to God, no matter what. I was sixteen years old when I began to discover my passion for people and church ministry. I listened to a sermon about God's invitation to Abraham to dream with Him. Genesis 15:5 says, "Then the Lord took Abram outside and said to him, 'Look up into the sky and count the starts if you can. That's how many descendants you will have!'" God wants you to dream with Him in regards to the future He has for your life. I trusted God would guide me along the path to fulfill the passions He had put inside of me. One year later, I received a groundbreaking prophetic word confirming the decisions I needed to make to pursue the purpose on my life. It was because of that confirming Word that I am on the path I am on today. You should desire to know God's will for your life, and God desires to reveal it to you. He just does not reveal the entire picture because we are called to walk by faith, and not by sight (2 Corinthians 5:7).

Identify Your Calling

> *For many are called, but few are chosen. (Matthew 22:14, ESV)*

You are called. You might even want to say it aloud. "I am called". You are called to change the World, but now the discovery of "how" is one that takes work. The few who are chosen are those who chose to run after their call. Let me help you do that!

Michael Hyatt, former CEO of Thomas Nelson Publishing House, teaches there are three areas you must assess when desiring to identify your calling. I believe that your career is a portion of your calling, but that does not fully encompass it in its entirety. When you identify your calling, which will be continually unveiled throughout your life, you will ultimately identify your career path. This is one of my favorite things to do for those that I serve in ministry. God has given me such a grace for helping others put language to their calling. Many have a sense or can recognize things they are passionate about, but cannot full communicate it to where someone else would be able to understand. Here are the three areas to assess to help you put language to what God is calling you to do for Him.

1. Passion: What do you love to do? What are you excited about doing at anytime, anywhere, with no money attached to it?
2. Proficiency: What are you skilled at doing?
3. Profitability: Is there a way to make money?

Michael goes on to say this, "If you have passion and competence without a market, you don't have a calling. You have a hobby. If you have passion and market without competence, you don't have a calling. You have a failure. If you have competence and a market without passion, you don't have a calling. You have boredom. It really does take all three components."

I chose full time ministry as my avenue to fulfill the passion and natural skill I had for helping people grow in God through biblical preaching and pastoring. I enhanced that skill by spending three years in bible college. Upon graduating I did not take the road that made sense to take, which would have been finding a full-time ministry position at a church as fast as I could. After sensing God's leading, I instead moved to Chicago to serve my Spiritual Father. I am currently a bi-vocational pastor. I spend my days as a Site Coordinator for an After School Program, and my evenings as a Student Ministry Pastor overseeing children's and youth ministry. This was not my original plan, but we are heading towards the future of what God has for us. Our main goal is to be obedient as He leads. This is just the beginning.

Write the vision down

Once you attain a basic understanding of your purpose then it is time to write a vision. In Habakkuk 2:2 it tells us, "To write the vision; make it plain on tablets, so he may run who reads it." Before we can write the vision, we must first get the vision. This requires prayer to seek God for revelations regarding major decisions you are supposed to make. Once God reveals to you key points, write them down. Many fail to write them down, and that is when you miss out on the ability to watch God work what He has shown you.

Destiny is a Journey, not a destination.

Growing up I enjoyed asking people a question you do not regularly hear kids asking. I would walk up to people at church and ask them, "Who are you in the bible?" Now, there is a reason why I asked this. My mom, who was the first to guide me to Christ, would have bible studies with us at home on the days we missed church. On one of those nights we studied the life of Joseph. While reading his account in the book of Genesis, I related so well with him. I became so excited, which is when my mom noticed, and then said; "You found yourself in the bible" I was so fascinated with this newfound concept of being able to find yourself in the bible. This has helped me navigate through some tough moments in life. Being misunderstood, not taken seriously, and rejected by those close to you is a snippet of what Joseph experienced. We learn through his story that your destiny is not a destination, but a journey. As you discover more about your purpose, continue to operate out of faith, which requires putting your trust in God.

Chapter 4

Foreign Exposure

My first roommates were my best friend from my hometown, and a really cool guy from Korea. Since then I have had over ten other roommates throughout my college and unmarried seasons of life. I did not begin to realize how much having different roommates helped prepare me for marriage until I got married. I had a great roommate experience, being able to take away something from each guy. I learned how to respect other people's stuff, pick up after myself, and resolve conflict. For some having a roommate may not be the best for your situation, but if you are able to then it could really help prepare you in regards to living with someone. Being exposed to other people's lifestyles and ways of doing things really helped me appreciate others. Even though you may not marry someone from another country, living with a diversity of people will help you see a different set of values and perspectives of life. We will dive more into this in another chapter.

Travel

Christian theologian, St. Augustine, states, "The world is a book and those who do not travel only read one page." I have had the privilege to travel to different countries on mission trips, and have to this date visited thirty different states. It is my goal to visit all fifty states and many more countries. Each place I have traveled has given me insight into other ways of living, different cultural values, and helped me build relationships with people unlike me. Some travel to places intrigued by their historical value or an attraction, but I love to go because of the people. I am a people watcher by profession. If you put me in a room with a lot of people do not expect me to stay focused because I will be observing everything and everyone. Each place I have visited, I have learned that the needs of people are synonymous. People need people. Get out and explore the world, I promise you will not regret it.

Chapter 5

Become a Best Friend

Friendships are one of the greatest assets in your life. If they are stewarded well, they can yield more harvest for you than anything else. The opposite is true when friendships are not taken care of. A person's greatest dysfunctions will most likely manifest in friendships, so this makes this the #1 way on my list of ways to prepare for marriage other than dating. It is through your friends that you will learn the most about yourself relationally. Become a student of yourself and your friends, and watch your relationship IQ begin to soar into new heights.

Friendship is the foundation of a great marriage. The components that make up a healthy friendship have nothing to do with attraction, intimacy, feelings, or compatibility, but everything to do with commitment via revelation and consistent communication. The friendship we find between David and Jonathan demonstrates commitment through revelation. First Samuel 18:1 tells us that, "As soon as [David] had finished speaking to Saul, the soul of Jonathan was knit to the soul of David, and Jonathan loved him as his own soul." It is here we see God working between David and Jonathan to connect them through the power of revelation. It is by revelation we are able to understand something that many see as natural, but we as believers see as supernatural. This allows us to depend on God versus depending on ourselves when it comes to who we allow into our lives.

We then find these words after the knitting of their souls in 1 Samuel 18:3, "Then Jonathan made a covenant with David, because Jonathan loved him as his own soul." The reaction to the revelation was commitment. In your friendships now, have you inquired unto God about their purpose in your life, or your purpose in theirs? Have you had a DTR (Define the Relationship) moment in order to bring some expectations for the friendship?

Communicate

Communication has always been and will always be one of the key components of a healthy relationship. My wife and I had a long distance relationship, so the majority of our time spent before marriage was over Skype or on the phone. It was one of the hardest things I had ever done, but it was so worth it. We really learned each other on so many levels, and when we did see one another the boundaries we had set in place kept us focused on enjoying one another communicatively versus physically. Any form of pre-marital sexual satisfaction in a relationship delays you from discovering key areas of the relationship such as the ability to commit, suitability, and agreement on future goals. Once you cross over into intimate physical acts outside of marriage, it is easy for it to become the major focus in the relationship.

Identify your strengths and weaknesses in relationships.

I consider relationships one of my strong points only because I recognize how significant they are to God. He really dealt with my heart towards committing and trusting people. As a kid I was very introverted, more than I am now. I feared labeling anyone as a "best friend," so I would just keep everyone at a friend level. This was because of my fear of giving someone so much freedom to hurt me. I kept people at a distance mainly using them for what they needed me for, but the moment I needed them I would resort to God versus running to friends. I know that seems backwards, but from my perspective God was perfect so He could never hurt or disappoint me. I would go even so far as to tell friends when they would want to spend quality time together that I needed to go be with God, which no one ever challenged, but man did God finally do it. He used Luke 10:27, "and He answered, 'You shall love the Lord your God with all your heart and with all your soul and with all your strength and with all your mind, and your neighbor as yourself.'" He said, "Jamal do you love me?" I said, "God, yes I love you." He then replied with, "Do you love yourself?" I answered Him, "Yes, God I love myself." He finally said, "If you truly loved yourself then you would be able to love others." It was not a "them" issue, it was a "me" issue. Because I did not value myself I feared being hurt and let down by others. This was a weakness I had to explain to my closest friends, who all helped me do better at valuing myself. I was the best at having hundreds of friends, but I feared having close friends that I depended upon. My weakness in relationships was my independence. By looking deep into your heart and examining your past you will find your flaws that require God to help bring an answer to why you are. So, if you are serious, stop reading and do the following:

1. Think of your last serious relationship. If never been in a serious relationship, think of a friendship.
2. What did you do that brought value to the relationship?
3. What did you do that made the relationship a challenge?

Learn how to deal with conflict with your friends.

We can all agree we were created for friendships. Even the most socially inept person has within them the desire to connect with another person. You can even think now about your closest friends and all of the amazing memories you have made together.

Friendship is a beautiful thing. I am grateful that I have been gifted with the abilities to love and relate with a variety of people. But, no matter how much you love people; you only have those select few in your life who you can consider as true friends, the friends that bring forth the power of Proverbs 27:17, "as iron sharpens iron, so a man sharpens the countenance of his friend." Or, the ones that pull out the virtue of Proverbs 17:17, "a friend loves at all times, and a brother is born for adversity." The bible is rather clear that friendships are vital for a productive and healthy life on Earth.

One day during college, a good friend of mine and I were walking to lunch. While walking, I started blabbing off and giving him a hard time about some things that happened in the past. Oblivious on my end, I continued on with no response from him the entire time. Later on that day, I get a text message from him asking me if we could chat for a bit. So we met up and he began to share with me some offense that had developed because of the things I had said earlier. I had no idea how what I was saying at the time had affected him so strongly. We came together that night and fully discussed it all. He explained his case, opening my eyes to how wrong I was for saying the things I had said. It actually really hurt me that I did not even recognize the tragedy of my words. I apologized and now we are rockin' and rollin'!

Every friendship will hit moments where one person does something to offend the other, and if you have not already developed an ability to be truthful it will eat you alive. The "two C's" of friendship go hand-in-hand: effective confrontation is the fruit of truthful communication. If my friend had not been truthful with me that day and communicated his heart, then he would have just gone on harboring the offense and I would have been completely oblivious to it. Many times, we try to avoid confrontation because we do not want to hurt the other person. But I promise you, you are hurting yourself MORE and robbing the other person. That is not fair!

It is now or never! Good friends do not come by in masses. It takes time. Every healthy and beneficial friendship is the fruit of effective confrontation. I like to call them "come to Jesus talks" because we end up confessing our hearts and it results in a stronger bond than before. James 5:16 even states we should "confess your sins to one another and pray for each other so that you may be healed." It is the most beautiful thing when the TRUTH comes out. John 8:32 says as much when Jesus said, "Then you will know the truth, and truth shall set you free."

Cherish your friends by keeping the 2 C's close in hand. Communication & Confrontation.

Without conflict in friendships there are not any opportunities for growth. Many run out of fear of offense or being hurt when conflict arises, but those are the ripe moments in friendships. If you do not learn how to confront conflict in a friendship, then marriage is going to be a challenge for you. Healthy communication is key for a smooth "come to Jesus" talk. I call it that because Christ is our Cornerstone, so when there is a disagreement we need to meet in the Center and move from there. Do not try to have friendships without Christ because it will lack revelation to make it through the moments that matter most.

Examine all your failed friendships and see why things went sour.

The best lessons learned are the ones that come from the moments in life where success is nowhere to be found. Failure has a plethora of effects on a person, and can sometimes be, in the right season, more valuable than success. Why? You not only learn what not to do the next time, but you also learn about a side of yourself that will prove invaluable for the future. I have a few friendships that did not pan out the way I desired for them too, but after examining what went wrong, it brought life to all of my future friendships.

Become a glass house for your close friends. (Transparency as a normal part of your life.)

Like I stated previously, one of my weaknesses is trusting others with the deep intricate parts of me because of my fear of being viewed as weak. When you are a leader you take on this superman mentality, living to save everyone, but easily forgetting about yourself. Transparency is the key that unlocks the door to a thriving, trustworthy covenant friendship. Allowing someone access into the parts of your life that even you are fearful of peering into is the beginning of shining the light on darkness. According to Ephesians 5:13, "But when anything is exposed by the light, it becomes visible." This must be for every secret you have, and will ever have. Do not wait, expose it. Any secrets you carry are not just between you and yourself, but you, yourself, and the devil. This is why God brings friends into our lives that we can build a covenant agreement to walk with us during hard times, and challenge us to grow. Becoming a glass house has been one of my most freeing joys due to my background of becoming a leader at such a young age. Many expect leaders to be perfect, or very close to it. I feared that if I was transparent about my issues people would call me a hypocrite, or I would make God look bad.

In a glass house you can see everything from every angle. I awoke from a dream with this concept burning in my heart to be developed into a teaching. In our generation, especially with the rise of social media, we are caught up sharing the highlights of our lives. You can, without hesitation, hide behind the highlight moments of your day, but who is invited into the dark moments? The Bible states in Proverbs, 18:1, "A man who isolates himself seeks his own desire; He rages against all wise judgment." Do not isolate yourself in order to prevent having to tell friends the whole truth. That is a strong spirit that causes you to masquerade like everything is okay, when actually your life can be in complete turmoil. You hurt yourself, and hurt those around you because they need the real you. If you do not have anyone in your life you trust to share the dark things about yourself then pray for God to send you someone. Your spouse will be your best friend, but they should not be your only friend.

Hiding Your Issues

> Do not lie to one another, seeing that you have put off the old self with its practices. (Colossians 3:9, ESV)

Before marriage, you and your future spouse will fall in love with one another's most striking attributes. After you get married, you will be tempted to hide your issues from your spouse. No one is perfect, and we will never be perfect. It is through the love of Christ we can be confident to be honest about our problems. Learning how to be transparent with your spouse in the beginning lays a solid foundation of trust. Marriage brings out the worst in you, in order for you to be the best for your spouse.

Proverbs 27:17 teaches us that as iron sharpens iron, so one person sharpens another. In order to understand the process by which iron is sharpened, we must see that it requires irons of different hardness. This explains why we find ourselves with those who are unlike us in different ways, but and yet value our need for them. When you marry, your spouse will be like you in some ways, but unlike you in others. The areas in which your spouse is strong will sharpen you, and where you are strong, you will sharpen your spouse. My temperament is described as choleric which is dominant, non-emotional, and aggressively goal oriented. My wife's temperament is a strong mixture of melancholic and phlegmatic. She is emotionally sensitive, and loves people to the core. Our goals in life are synonymous, but our personalities are not. We sharpen each other in many ways, truly refining our "rough areas" in order to make each other who God created us to be.

Ask your close friends what are areas of your character need development every 3-6 months.

This can only be done after you have consistently become a glass house. One of my best friends sends me a text message at the half point of each year, stating, "What areas of my life do you believe I could improve in?" Now, I know that is a group text, but I also know he only sent it to those that he knows, know him well enough to answer truthfully. Let's do it right now! Think of four or five people who know your life and text them stating, "Based on your time spent with me and your honest opinion, what are some improvements I could make in my character or life as a whole"? Take those answers and get to work.

Section II

Chapter 6

Work Hard

I was on the phone with my dad a few weeks ago after attending a business conference. He asked me how I enjoyed it, which lead into an eye opening conversation about my grandparents. He began to tell me how my grandmother only had a 4th grade education, and my grandfather had a 6th grade education, but had multiple jobs and worked extremely hard. My dad took on their work ethic. It was because of this ethic he learned from his parents that I can say growing up we never lacked for anything. A great work ethic is such an attractive quality that cannot be learned in a day, but has to be developed over time. There is a lot more to it than spending long hours at work.

It is having a motivation to accomplish goals on a consistent basis. It is having the ability to say no to distractions, and yes to obedience. You may ask, what does me working hard have to do with preparing for marriage? Everything! Your marriage will require this ability due to the many challenges causing you at times to want to throw in the towel. Those who work hard have a determination to get to an expected end which requires a commitment to never quit! The bible teaches very extensively on this subject because our God is a hard worker!

> *But Jesus answered them, "My Father is working until now, and I am working." (John 5:16, ESV)*

> *Work hard and become a leader; be lazy and become a slave. (Proverbs 12:24, NLT)*

> *Whoever works his land will have plenty of bread, but he who follows worthless pursuits lacks sense. (Proverbs 12:11, ESV)*

How to Develop a Solid Work Ethic

Start your day strong. When you wake up in the morning, what is the first thing you do? Is it something that is planned, or are you automatically allowing your day to determine what you do versus you determining what you do. By starting your day off strong, you are taking control of your day which will have a domino effect on the rest of your day. On Sunday evenings I plan out my entire week with agendas and goals. Each night I look over what I have for the next day so I can be prepared to tackle it the moment I wake up. It is up to you to plan what you do when you first wake up. It has been suggested by motivational speaker and self-help expert, Brendan Burchard that doing something for self-first each day helps you focus better on each task you have to complete. Starting your day off strong is a sure way to jump-start yourself into developing a strong work ethic.

Set Deadlines. For the most part every job requires some sort of deadline, goal, or quota that must be met in order to track your job performance. We are accustomed to them in the workplace, but when it comes to our personal lives it is easy to march to the beat of everyone else's drum rather than our own. Do not just set goals, set deadlines. You are the CEO of your life, but remember you are not the Founder. Make sure your goals are in alignment with the vision God has given you for your life. Once those goals are set then make sure a deadline is put in place for them. Have someone keep you accountable for your goals.

Do Hard Things. "For I can do all things through Christ who strengthens me", stated in Philippians 4:13 is a staple verse for most Christians. We quote it, memorize it, and occasionally shout it out when life is challenging us most. This verse is an invitation to do things bigger than yourself. I have always been a day dreamer. You hear a lot about those who have these fantastic dreams at night. Well, I had a roommate that dreamed deep prophetic dreams each night. You do not hear a lot about daydreamers other than they are not able to pay attention because they drift off to somewhere else. That is me! I remember times as a little boy riding in the car with my parents staring out the window into the sky and I would begin to day dream about my future. I saw the many things I could never imagine now being able to accomplish them on my own. As I grew older I learned how to dream with God. This led me to start writing down the dreams he had placed in my heart. One day He said to me, "Jamal these dreams will require you to do hard things, but they will seem easy to you because I will be doing it through you." All I had to do was believe God and take the risks to do it. God cannot force you to anything, but He can empower you.

"For it is God working in you, giving you the desire and power to do what pleases Him." (Philippians 2:13, NLT)

Be Motivated by Purpose not Emotions. In the open verse of the Book of Joshua we find the retelling of Moses death.

"Moses my servant is dead. Now therefore arise, go over this Jordan, you and all this people, into the land that I am giving to them, to the people of Israel. Every place that the sole of your foot will tread upon, I have given to you, just as I promised to Moses" (Joshua 1:2-3, ESV)

This verse teaches us about God's desire to direct us according to His purpose for our lives. He gives Joshua the command to go into the land that He is giving, and even encourages them later in the passage that He will never leave them nor forsake them. As you are setting yourself to work harder be sure to be driven by the purpose of God. The reason you are driven by the purpose of God is because it is your ultimate desire to be pleasing to God. This is the center of having a work ethic that never fails. When God is the center of attention He will be your stretching factor strengthening you to handle any challenges.

Stay away from lazy people. Second Thessalonians 3:6-10 states, "And now, dear brothers and sisters, we give you this command in the name of our Lord Jesus Christ: Stay away from all believers who live idle lives and do not follow the tradition they received from us. For you know that you ought to imitate us. We were not idle when we were with you. We never accepted food from anyone without paying for it. We worked hard day and night so we would not be a burden to any of you." The church at Thessalonica was a church full of young, new believers. Each epistle written by the Apostle Paul addressed each churches specific challenges and those issues needing to be focused on. We see him here addressing that issue of laziness. He encourages them to stay away from any believer that is not living according to the tradition they had set in place. That tradition was simply working hard. Those being called out were not just sitting at home doing nothing with their time, but later in the passage he addresses them meddling in others people business. In verse 11 Paul says, "Yet we hear that some of you are living idle lives, refusing to work and meddling in other people's business." This makes it clear that they were not living their lives on purpose, but wasting God's given time on selfish gain. If you have friends like this in your life be very careful with how much access they have to your life. I have made some very intentional moves in this season of my life to spend more quality time with people ahead of me in life. Those who are running at my level are essential, but it takes effort to acquire people doing more than you.

Take the Day Off. This personally has been a challenging task for me. It is much easier for me to work hard then it is to rest from the work of my labor. This is a "trust in God" issue. When you are not able to rest from work then it reveals your dependency on achieving success through your own hands rather than God's hands. God established a pattern in the very beginning that has either been abused or neglected. In Genesis 2:2 we read that "by the seventh day God had finished the work he had been doing; so on the seventh day he rested from all his work." Once you establish the ethic of working hard, you must understand why you must rest from your work.

Resting biblically is known as the Sabbath. Taking a day of rest is not just an idea God came up with, it is a commandment. Yes, even now being in the new covenant we will can be guided by the Ten Commandments. Christ dying on the cross fulfilled the Ten Commandments enabling us to be free from the penalty of breaking God's laws. Because it is now a principle that means it can be applied any way you desire to do so. Exodus 31:16 states, "The people of Israel must keep the Sabbath day by observing it from generation to generation. This is a covenant obligation for all time" (NLT). All time is forever! Today we have business days, which is Monday-Friday. Then, the weekends for majority major corporations are off days. Work schedules vary from each job so choose a day of the week that you are off from work to rest from the week. On your rest day you do simply that, rest. Rest can include anything that is not considered work. Include in your time with God room to thank Him for the many blessings in your life, and worship Him for his faithfulness. You can spend quality time with family, go do your favorite hobby, and end your day with prayer. We do this so we can honor God for giving us the ability to work, and also honor ourselves.

Chapter 7

Identify Your Temptations

"Lead us not into temptation, but deliver us from the evil one." (Matthew 6:13, ESV)

The temptations in your life are no different from what others experience. And God is faithful. He will not allow the temptation to be more than you can stand. When you are tempted, He will show you a way out so that you can endure. (1 Corinthians 10:13, NLT)

Both of these verses indicate that temptation is a part of everyday life, and we need to be aware of what our temptations are. The more you starve something the more the desire for it weakens. This is how temptation works, if you focus in on it then you are giving it more power, but if you take authority over it and move forward you will see victory. By examining your past "missing of the mark" you can learn what your fleshly weaknesses are. Identify your temptations and set up a system for when you sense you are weak. There is a heavily taught acronym called, H.A.L.T, which stands for hungry, angry, lonely, or tired. I learned of this acronym while reading a book called, "Every Man's Battle". This book was a catalyst in my life due to my exposure to pornography at the tender age of ten. This opened the door to the spirit of lust in my life, and it went from a temptation to an addiction. It brought so much shame and I was disgusted with my thoughts, and actions. It was not until I identified this weakness and exposed it to leaders in my life, and that allowed the healing power of Christ to overtake the desire for it. But, even though the power of sin was broken, temptation still exists. I had to learn what triggered me, and to stay away from certain movies in order to protect my mind. Let's dive deeper into temptation because it will play a major role in your future marriage. You will need revelation on this subject to power through weak moments, and also to have grace on your future spouse for their weaknesses. Here's a short story to help you breathe a little as we power through the hard topic of temptation and sin.

> "Once upon a time, four pastors were spending a couple of days at a cabin. In the evening they decided to tell each other their biggest temptation. The first pastor said, "Well, it's kind of embarrassing, but my big temptation is bad pictures. Once I even bought a copy of the Sports Illustrated Swimsuit Edition." "My temptation is worse," said the second pastor "It's gambling. One Saturday instead of preparing my sermon I went to the race track to bet on horses." "Mine is worse still," said the third pastor. "I sometimes can't control the urge to drink. One time I actually broke into the sacramental wine." The fourth pastor was quiet. "Brothers, I hate to say this," he said, "but my temptation is worst of all. I love to gossip-and

if you guys will excuse me, I'd like to make a few phone calls!"

God Is Not the Tempter

James tells us to remember that "when you are being tempted do not say, God is tempting me" (1:13).God is never tempted to do wrong, and he never tempts anyone else. God will never place something in front of you in order to make you fall. That is how Satan works. Matthew records in 4:1, "Then Jesus was lead up by the Spirit into the wilderness to be tempted by the devil". God tries us in order to for us to be perfected, but Satan tempts us that we might sin.

The Purpose of temptation

James 1:2-3 says, "Dear brothers and sisters, when troubles come your way, consider it an opportunity for great joy because you know that the testing of your faith produces perseverance. Let perseverance finish its work so that you may be complete, not lacking anything. God certainly has a purpose for temptation." He first desires to reveal us to ourselves. Each time I have fallen short of God's standard it revealed to me what I am capable of when I take control rather than continuously staying rooted in Christ. Acknowledging where you are weak makes room for God to supplement you with power. Another purpose of temptation is to give us an opportunity to be built stronger in God. Think back to a moment where you were being tempted, and you overcame. You felt stronger, encouraged in your Spirit that nothing could stop you. It is the exact opposite when we give into temptation. We feel weakened, condemned and mad at ourselves. The voice of condemnation can be very challenging we will deal with this in a later chapter.

Temptation in Marriage

Temptation in marriage is a reality that many hope will not affect their supernatural love story. You are human before you get married and you will be human after you get married. For the rest of your life in this fallen world temptation will be there. If you do not learn the ins and outs of temptation before marriage, then it will be a problem within it. The devil surely hated you before you got married, but now he really hates you. He hates everything marriage represents, and has set himself out to destroy the foundation on which it stands. You must be prepared because whatever temptations you failed to master during your season of singleness will be intensified in marriage. This is why it is imperative to take this season seriously; to grow your roots deep in Christ for the killing of your flesh. Your life and the life of your spouse is made one in marriage, so now what affects you will affect your spouse.

Chapter 8

Develop a Strong Relationship with Mentors & Spiritual Parents

Plans fail for the lack of counsel, but with many advisers they succeed. (Proverbs 15:22, NIV)

This may be my personal favorite way to prepare for marriage other than dating simply because if it had not been for my spiritual father, Dr. Matthew Stevenson, I probably would still be single. I believe strongly in having support through life from either a mentor, pastor, or mature family member. Jesus had the twelve disciples, Elijah had Elisha, and Paul had Timothy. These are all biblical examples of the spiritual parenting paradigm. Attempting to do life without the assistance, support, and encouragement of someone who has walked the same path you are on is not wise. Every child needs a father, and every child of God needs a Spiritual Father. God brought Matthew Stevenson into my life when I was first being awakened to the call on my life at the age of 17. We had no connections and lived in two different parts of the United States. I stumbled upon an article he wrote on the Internet. I emailed him spilling my guts about wanting to better understand who God was calling me to be. He actually responded and answered all the questions he could. That eventually developed into him checking in on me throughout my high school years. Two years later while in college he invited me to come speak at his conference in Chicago, which is where we met face to face for the first time. Two years after that, when I graduated from college, we both felt this heavy need for me to spend a season in Chicago with him and to serve under his vision. I obeyed the leading of God and left my family, friends, and all I knew to move to Chicago. This had to be one of the most magnanimous leaps of faith I had ever taken. It was not easy at all. I read the story of Abraham every night when I went to sleep to remind me of the blessing that comes when you trust and follow God. Well, three years later I am still here. I am now married which would not have happened without him. Our relationship is a true supernatural example of God putting people into your life who will push, love, and support you into purpose. I would not be half the man I am today if it was not for his obedience, and God's faithfulness!

A mentor is someone who teaches you a specific skill during a specific season of your life. I have many people in my life whom I consider mentors, for they have helped me navigate through different scenarios with wisdom and to home in my various set of skills. One of my mentors I give credit to for helping me take our website, Marriedandyoung.com to another level. He saw the potential it had when my wife and I first started it, and from his experience as Director of Marketing for a multi-million dollar education firm, he offered his expertise on that subject which changed the trajectory we were on. By having respected people in your life whom you can be honest with and allowing them some authority to help steer your life into the right direction; you can mature at a much quicker rate.

The bible states in 1 Corinthians 4:15, "For though you have countless guides in Christ, you do not have many father's. For I became you father in Christ Jesus through the gospel." This is very true for our day due to the many leaders guiding people to Christ, but not accepting the important dimension of fathering. Spiritual parenting is not limited to males, but also females can be a spiritual parent. If you do not have someone in your life whom you can consider a spiritual parent, then find a person you respect to ask them if they can mentor you. A spiritual Father or Mother is one who has committed to helping you become who God has created you to be. This is one of the most valuable relationships due to the longevity and authority God gives spiritual parents. Just like you have natural parents that help raise you up to maturity, you need to have a spiritual parent that can walk with you during your development years as a believer. I have a very healthy relationship with my natural Father, which helped develop a healthy relationship with my spiritual Father due to not having wounds or bitterness towards authority. It is very possible for your natural parents to also be your spiritual parents.

These types of relationships are pivotal for growing in God beyond your limitations because you will gain impartation from leaders who have walked the same path you are on, and overcame! If you do not have either a mentor or spiritual parent, ask God to reveal to you someone in your life that could fit that role. Do not be quick to allow anyone to be your spiritual parent because that is a God given relationship. Trust and wait on God. With mentors, go after them as you see fit for what your season requires.

Chapter 9

Become Interdependent

A person who is interdependent is not solely dependent on others, nor are they solely dependent on themselves, but rather understands they need others to thrive in life. When we come out of the womb we are fully dependent on our parents, and the goal is to learn how to do life on our own while being mutually interdependent upon others. This quality is best seen in those that are not too prideful to ask for help or support, and are able to do the same for others. Every husband feels esteemed when their wives depend on them, but they treasure a woman they can depend on as well. This goes for the physical as well as the emotional. We all need to be able to take care of ourselves financially, but also able to receive support from others when needed. Also, being emotionally secure, but able to reach out when you are having a hard time. My issue with interdependence was I knew how to let others depend on me because I was a natural leader, but I did not know how to depend on others. Even now being married I still have a hard time depending on my wife. This has been something we have had to take grain-by-grain. This shows you that when you get married, you will not be perfect. You will actually realize even more how imperfect you are.

Practice submitting.

Submission IS NOT, I repeat, IS NOT just for women or even for wives. It seems the moment we see the word we automatically turn it towards a marriage term for a wife. The reason submission is an issue within marriage is because it was not intentionally practiced before marriage. Submitting can simply be described as surrendering. Surrendering begins and ends with Christ. Our first major surrender should be when we surrender our heart and mind to King Jesus. Once we surrender to Him, we never have to fight our own battles or defend ourselves, because He now does that for us. Psalm 37:7-8, "Surrender yourself to the Lord, and wait patiently for Him. Do not worry about evil people who prosper about their wicked schemes. Stop your anger! Turn from your rage! Do not envy others—it only leads to harm." In the Kingdom, one who is able to surrender is one whose identity does not lie within themselves.

Chapter 10

Serve at Your Local Church.

Serve at your local church.

I love to serve! It has been such a lifeline for me through my years of growing as a Christian. When God began to deal with me on my selfish ways, I asked Him how I could become more selfless. Well, those who are selfless, are servants. Christ when He arrived on the scene stated boldly, "I have not come to be served, but that I might serve" (Mark 10:45). How powerful is that? The King of the Universe, Lord of All, and Creator of Mankind coming with one agenda, to serve us. How much more should we desire to serve Him? And, there is no better place to do it than the place where souls are saved, disciples are made, and communities are changed.

Serving your local church not only benefits your church, but more importantly it benefits you. By serving you discover more about yourself in an environment perfect for growth and the unmasking of your real issues. Yes, the church is not for the perfect, but for those who accept they need help. Servanthood is a response to God's goodness and the responsibility that comes once we become an ambassador for His Kingdom. Many deal with the issue of self-centeredness and selfishness, for which serving is the best remedy.

When we began highlighting couples on the Married and Young Facebook page, we saw a consistent flow of stories come through. Those stories all detailed how they met at church while serving in a particular ministry. Serving allows you to meet new people in a safe environment where trust is easily established.

Become a mentor

I have been a pastor for about seven years now. This has allowed me a first-hand view of the power of investing into others' lives. This is another opportunity to give back to God what He has invested in you by supporting someone else with life skills you have acquired or just provide encouragement through life. The same qualities it takes to be a mentor will be used in your marriage. My wife and I mentor each other at different moments all the time. The most awesome thing about a mentor is they require nothing back. Are you at a place in your life where you are able to give without requiring anything in return? You can consider it a certainty that your future spouse will demand this grace in your life.

Section III

Chapter 11

Acknowledge what You have to Offer

Can we be honest for a second? No one wants to marry someone that is not bringing value into the relationship? Every time I teach on this topic, I begin by saying, "Do not marry someone for their potential because that is NOT guaranteed." It is so dangerous to fall in love with what someone could become if they...finish the sentence. That is basic witchcraft because you are now forcing that person to become something they possibly do not have it within their power to become. That brings us to you.

What do you have to bring into a relationship that makes it even more valuable? This includes but is not limited to: maturity, life experiences, purity, finances, education, life skills, career, relationships, and the list could go on. When I met my wife there were the non-negotiable qualities about her that I knew my wife must possess before we married which were much more valuable to me than degrees, finances, and the rest. No one is perfect so this requires much flexibility. You also cannot require a person to have things that you never took the time to acquire as well. What are you bringing to the table and what qualities do you desire your future spouse to possess before you marry?

Now, when you begin to assess what you are bringing to the table you have to be honest about the things you do not have. This is a fun component of Natasha and I's story. We met online via Facebook, so we had built this amazing relationship all before we had ever seen one another in person, other than pictures on Facebook. Well, the time came for us to meet face to face. She agreed to come visit Chicago and also attend my churches annual World Changer's Conference. A few days before she was to depart, I had to be honest with her about something that I was very insecure about. It was my height. I could tell she was not short, but did not know exactly how tall she was either. So, finally after much beating around the bush, I was honest with her. Due to how much build up I did she had come to the resolve of saying, "You're not a midget, are you?" I said, "OH NO, I am not a midget, LOL."I said, "I am 5'7". She quickly replied back with, "Oh, that's not a problem, I am 5'6"."Most women desire taller men, and I have had so many cases where I was interested in a girl, but she desired someone taller. That allowed Natasha to be honest about her insecurity of not having a college degree. This night was healing for the both of us as we were fearful about how one another would respond to our insecurities. Do not be fearful of what you do not have, but trust that God will pair you with someone who will love what you do have to offer.

Skills

What skills do you have that can be utilized for daily life—extra streams of income, or serving others? Daily life can include, but does not need to be limited to skills with cooking, fixing things, being creative, building, or speaking. The list could go on. Any of these can make way for extra streams of income if one of those skills were taken to a mastery level.

Character

Your character is important. To be the right person can be one of the most valuable assets that you bring into a relationship. This is something that requires intentionality in order for it to be developed. Are you easily angered, cannot forgive quickly, talk negative behind people's back? Or, are you a loving, caring, kind-hearted, forgiving, speak well of others, and are someone others wand to be around?

Education

The discipline to attain a high level degree is noteworthy, and also brings value into the relationship. An education opens doors for careers that would not have been available otherwise. I better explain the place of education is another chapter.

Relationships

Just like I explained in the chapter earlier, your relationships will make or break who God has called you to be. I did not have to drop any of my friends when I got married because they became even more necessary once I crossed over. Why? Because, they were helping me become a better man. Healthy relationships that transition smoothly into your marriage will continue to help you develop and grow. Also, it is all about who you know. It was prophesied to my wife before she met me that her future husband would have established relationships that she would inherit. I never viewed my relationships with not only close friends, but mentors and leaders as an inheritance until she told me that prophecy. Do not isolate yourself during this season, get out and cultivate meaningful, purpose-centered relationships.

Chapter 12

Pray For Your Future Spouse

Each night during my quiet time with God I would always end with a few short prayers covering my wife (whom I had not met yet). I did not make requests about what I wanted her to be, but I prayed over her knowing she was already somewhere fully created. I would pray protective prayers over her, and ask that God would continue to push her into purpose knowing we would meet one day. I made sure not to allow that to be the majority of my prayer time because during singleness your main priority should be the development of yourself, and your relationship with God. Praying for your spouse gives God full control, and will encourage you during your season of waiting with patience. I thank God He encouraged me to do this, because it was the very prayers that I prayed over my future wife that helped me recognize that Natasha was the one I had been praying for all those years.

Your future spouse is a real person. When I came to understand that God was impressing upon me to pray for my future spouse, it changed everything. Instead of me praying for specific things I had no control over, such as certain physical attributes, type of personality, or even how we would meet, I prayed for who she was becoming. I knew God had someone for me that was living and breathing, so that person needed prayers that would help her versus pray for things I or she could not change. Here are four prayers that will help your spouse as God is preparing you both for one another.

Growing in Their Relationship with God

This is the most important prayer your future spouse needs. Praying they are growing in their relationship with God will result in them making wise decisions, their heart staying clear of build up from life, and them discovering who God has called them to be. The first thing I prayed for each time I covered my future spouse in prayer was that she was not only a lover of God, but proactively growing in her relationship with God.

Progressing in their Purpose for their life

The purpose of God is on your life, and your future spouse's life. If they are living their life according to that, then in the right time your paths will cross. I teach heavily on this subject because it is the desire of every person, whether they are believers or not, they all want direction towards their "purpose". Your prayers for them to be progressing in their purpose will assist them in choosing a career path in alignment with what their passions are.

Establishing a strong support system for success

Who your future spouse's friends are plays a major role in how they conduct their life, and the mentors or lack thereof will be a solidifying factor for success. I prayed over my wife's inner and outer circle of relationships. That they were helping her be a better person, and supporting her in all her endeavors.

Protection from counterfeits

A counterfeit is someone that comes very close to the real thing, but in reality is not. They may be attractive, but a bum with no job. Or they could be a well-established person making great money, but does not have an active relationship with God. This prayer became more important as I began to recognize counterfeits arising in my life. Women who peaked my curiosity, but there I had no peace to pursue. If I would have been anxious, I would have possibly pursued, but I felt the confidence to wait on God. Now, being married, and hearing my wife say she prayed this over me gives me confirmation I had help. My wife has many stories of guys being interested in her, but she turned them all down either because of dreams from God, an unsettlement in her spirit, or the relationship not progressing. I was my wife's first committed relationship, her first kiss, and the rest is history. Those prayers worked!

Chapter 13

Financial Intelligence

Okay, I know you are tired of hearing, "you need to know how to budget before you get married", or anything with the word budget in it. This point is not about learning how to budget because honestly I want you to be able to buy your Starbucks, go on that vacation, or purchase those new jeans. Budgeting could help you eventually attain it, but it would take a lot longer than just having the financial intelligence to create extra streams of revenue in order to have the freedom to make those purchases. Yes, a monthly spending plan is essential for growth, but it means nothing if you do not have any intelligence on how to capitalize on your savings. Financial intelligence requires much reading and exposing yourself to great minds who have learned the rules of finance! Financial intelligence will benefit your spouse more than just having the ability to stick to a monthly budget. Before we jump into the how to of developing your financial intelligence, I want you to ask yourself this question. "What is my relationship with money?"

Develop the discipline of having a monthly spending plan

It is said that finances is one of the top causes of divorce today. Many think once they get married money will eventually work itself out. WRONG! When you are single it is easy to get away with a budget-less life, but once you are married it is one of the most necessary **disciplines** needed. I encourage you to start a budget now, and do some study on personal finances. Luke 14:28 states it so perfectly, "don't begin to build until you have considered the cost." If you can learn this concept while single you will bypass many arguments during budget time and your spouse will thank you for it. By developing a discipline of having a monthly spending plan you will then become consistent with putting money where it belongs. Your bills will be paid on time, you will give your tithes regular, and you will invest more into your future.

Give generously

Giving is the heart of the kingdom and reveals the heart of man. I believe with all my heart many of the blessings I received, such as having the majority of our wedding being paid for, never lacking financially, or God ordained opportunities for multiple streams of income all stem from the generous giving I did before I married and still do now being married. I remember a dear friend of mine was getting married and I just had a sincere desire to pay for his honeymoon. Yes, I did do it out of the faith believing God that someone would pay for mine once I got married. Well, the majority of our wedding was covered through generous blessings, but our honeymoon came fully out of my pocket. Not being ungrateful, but the thought did come to my mind as to why my seed sowed did not reap a harvest there. Well, fast forward to almost a year later (the present). A few weeks ago a friend of mine called me asking if we were planning our 1 year anniversary to which I replied, yes! He then said, God laid it on my heart to pay for you and Natasha's 1 year anniversary vacation. I almost did two back flips because not at all was I expecting him to say that.

Sowing and reaping is a biblical principle you can be sure God stands by, but He does not do it on your terms. I encourage you to develop the passion for giving generously to others and watch God work on your behalf. Second Corinthians 4:12 says that "whatever you give is acceptable if you give it eagerly. And give according to what you have, not what you don't have."

Pay down debt

Making and sticking to a plan to pay down your debt is an act of love towards your future spouse. Even though when you marry your spouse, they also marry everything that comes with you. They should not be penalized for your lack of discipline to work as hard as possible to pay down debt. I do understand there are debts that takes years to eradicate i.e. school, car loans, etc. I am not saying you should not have any debt going into a marriage, but you should make it a priority before you marry to pay it down as much as possible. Do not wait to marry someone with the plan to then start paying down your debt. I have talked with a few unmarried women some with over $100,000 in school loans and another with a horrific credit history fearful of a potential husband being turned away due to their financial situation. This is a major issue for both men and women today due to the increase in need for school loans and a hard economy preventing the paying down of those loans. My encouragement is to learn how to manage your money wisely making way for you to become disciplined in your finances.

Pay your tithes

After watching my mom tithe my entire life, I was so excited to do it once I started making my own money. God has shown Himself faithful in this area of my life more times than I can count. I remember my first time seeing my older brother ride his bike without training wheels. It was so cool, and I instantly wanted to do the same. I jumped on it and crashed. My dad came over to me and said, "Jamal you need to learn how to ride on the training wheels before you move on to the big boy bike." I would practice every day until I felt I was ready to do it again. This is the same with tithing. God has set up that the starting point is 10% of your income, but that is only training for where He truly desires to take you which is giving over and above the minimum. Second Corinthians 9:7 states, "You must each decide in your heart how much to give. And don't give reluctantly or in response to pressure. For God loves a person who gives cheerfully." My goal was not to stay on the training wheels, but to one day be able to ride freely without any assistance. I believe with all of my heart the reason I have never lacked is because I have faithfully been a tither and giver. From full college scholarships, vehicles paid off, never not had a job, supernatural wedding, and much more have been the fruit of my, and now our, faithfulness. Have there been hard times? Absolutely. But, those hard times simply reminded us of who are source of joy is. Jesus. This is God's heart for your tithe.

Chapter 14

Learn Yourself

Marriage is the process by which two become ONE! Well, it is a lot easier for those two to become one when they understand the parts of themselves that refuses to surrender. When you know yourself well, you can acknowledge where you need Christ to overcome your weaknesses with His strength. It makes the merger of two individuals a piece of cake. The first few years of marriage are the most difficult for those who refuse to give up and surrender to God's inventive method for Christ-likeness. Learning yourself is best done in the environment of healthy friendships, volunteering at your local church, and allowing the Word to reveal those hidden things in your heart fighting against selfless living. Stay true to who God created you to be. You are His masterpiece and He takes great pride in you. Every second spent comparing yourself to others robs you of precious moments you could be thanking God for what He has invested in you. The part of you that is most unlike others is what makes you valuable to those around you. We need the real you!

Learn when to say yes, and when to say NO. (Self-control)

I am seeing that one of the major problems for our society today is self-gratification, or the inability to tell yourself NO, and to acknowledge when something is not good for you, is the cause of...

1. JACKED UP relationships because I just like the way he/she makes me "feel" and because "I have needs too"
2. JACKED UP eating habits because "it tastes so good." You cannot eat it, if you do not buy it!
3. JACKED UP work ethics because "I do not feel like going to work today" This is just LAZY!
4. JACKED UP finances because "well, it is on sale", or better yet, "I get paid at the end of the month, so it is cool, charge it to my credit card." Your children are going to SUFFER because of your choices today.
5. JACKED UP authority issues because "no one can tell me what to do." I GUARANTEE you will be BROKE and a JOKE trying to be successful if you are not teachable.
6. JACKED UP God issues because, "I'm too tired to pray, or I don't understand the bible."

The list could go on...unless a person learns how to tell themselves NO, they will FOREVER be controlled by destructive desires. Self-control is a FRUIT of the Spirit, which means it cannot be done WITHOUT God! This is what separates those who make it to the end with a lasting legacy, and those who do not.

What do you do to have fun?

Your hobby not only will bless you, but it may help you find your spouse. I have met so many couples who met while doing something they loved to do. Hobbies are one of the greatest intersections for building relationships. Make it a priority to first acknowledge what you like to do, then make plans to do it.

Learn more about your love language

Gary Chapman's book, *The 5 Love Languages,* is one of the most popular relationship books written in our day. In it, Dr. Gary masterfully explains five languages that we all use to communicate or receive love from. The five are:

1. Physical touch.
2. Words of Affirmation.
3. Acts of service.
4. Gifts.
5. Quality time.

Identifying which love language is yours can be accomplished very quickly by examining what comes natural to you in relationships, and what you desire most in a relationship. It is usual that how you love is what you desire the most. Also, your love language changes as you change throughout different seasons of life.

Questions to learn more about yourself

From my experience one of the most time worthy investments that have yielded more money and value into my life has been the investment of learning who I am in Christ. The more I understand about my God created DNA make up, the more I am able to unlock keys to prophetic perspective about my destiny. I ask myself these DNA unlocking questions:

1. What invigorates me?
2. What do I naturally spend much of my time doing?
3. What type of people do I naturally draw to?
4. What type of people do I not like being around?
5. What are my unhealthy habits? Why do I that?
6. Why do my closest friends keep me as their friend?
7. What do I go to sleep thinking about and wake up thinking about?
8. What things bring me to complete boredom?
9. What do people say about me after meeting me for the first time?
10. What would 1 week of my life look like if I could do anything without distractions?
11. What have been my most challenging moments of my life?
12. Where have I wasted the most time?
13. What prophetic words spoken over me as child have come to pass?
14. What am I proficient at naturally? What would that skill look like developed?
15. Who are the most inspiring people to me? Why?

Chapter 15

Stay Healthy

One of the realities of life is your body's metabolism slows down the older you get. Before, you could possibly get away with eating fast food a few times a week, or ice cream every night before you went to sleep. This will not last forever because your metabolism will slow down causing those unhealthy habits to catch up with you. "Metabolism is the breakdown of metabolic fuels we have in the diet," explains Christopher Newgard, director of the Sarah W. Stedman Nutrition and Metabolism Center at Duke University Medical School. "The primary nutrients in foodstuff can be classified as fats, proteins or carbohydrates. I think of metabolism as the way the cells, organs and tissues in our bodies handle those kinds of fuels." Healthyliving.msn.com. In other words, it is not just about burning calories, but about eating healthy foods that help us maintain an energized body!

Being healthy is not just about being attractive, but also about valuing yourself. If I gave my little nephew candy every day, he will never turn me down, but that is selfish of me. He is not mature enough to know what is good or bad for him. You are mature enough now to accept that eating out every day, or having sweets for dinner is probably not the best for your body.

Take care of yourself because how you value yourself will determine how you others value you.

Learn how to Cook

Please, whether you are a male or female do not take this skill for granted. Our generation prides itself on having the entire McDonald's $1.00 menu memorized, or being able to get full on $2.50. Eating out consistently is not only very costly, but can be equally unhealthy. Learning how to cook saves you money, builds better relationships, and gives you control over what you are putting into your body. Natasha and I rotate cooking days in order for both us to share that responsibility due to us both having day jobs. I enjoy cooking, and Natasha does as well, but we both have different dishes we like to experiment with which makes it so much fun when it comes time to eat. Side note here: I am a huge advocate for eating dinner at the table. The dinner table is one of the lost vehicles for great conversation.

Have dinner parties

One of the qualifications of a leader in a church is that they must be hospitable desiring to open their home to others. A healthy marriage requires healthy relationships. Some of the best times we have spent with other couples is around our dinner table. I am from the South, so I really believe in the power of eating dinner together. A dinner party does not begin with cooking, nor does it begin with cleaning your home. It begins with the desire to serve others. My wife does it better than anyone I know. I get so excited to invite couples over to my home because I know I have a wife that shares the same passion of hospitality. Start now by planning a night for friends to come over, even if you are not a chef, delegate the cooking to others who enjoy it. The main purpose is to learn the joy of serving others.

Work Out

Working out is a discipline that, once mastered and made a part of your daily life, can become as easy as brushing your teeth. (Hopefully that is easy for you!)It does not require a lot, but simply being consistent. Thirty minutes every day can go so far. Find a routine that works for your schedule and stick to it. Even if you do not have the money for a gym membership, there are a myriad of indoor and outdoor activities that can help you stay fit. Make it a priority because you draw what you are.

Section IV

Chapter 16

Examine Your Cultural Values

Whether you are from the inner city of Chicago, to the swamps of Louisiana, or Sunny California, within your home there was an established culture. That culture dictated how you did certain things and what you valued. My wife and I come from similar backgrounds. Both our parents were hard working, African-Americans, and had a foundational belief in God. Even with all those similarities we still have things that were done differently in our homes that we have had to learn how to adjust to. By first recognizing what is a valuable to you, then you will be able to value what is important to someone else.

Gender Roles

1. What is the role of the husband in the home?
2. What is the role of the wife in the home?

Parenting

1. What are the responsibilities of a Father?
2. What are the responsibilities of a Mother?

3. What do you think about stay-at-home Mothers?
4. What do you think about stay-at-home Fathers?

Education

1. What do you consider an adequate education?
2. Is an education a requirement for success?
3. Are people with a college degree smarter than those without a college degree?
4. Will your child have to go to college?

Faith

1. How important is a relationship with God in your marriage?
2. Is a healthy marriage possible without God?
3. How involved do you need to be in your local church?
4. How do you envision the husband leading his family spiritually?

Finances

1. What is your relationship with money?
2. What do you consider needs?
3. What do you consider wants?
4. Do you believe in tithing regularly?

Chapter 17

Deal With Your Chatterbox

"For as he thinks, in his heart, so is he..." (Proverbs 23:7a, AMP)

My second semester of college I was awarded a full scholarship. This allowed me to quit my job as a waiter, and pursue ministry. I was hired on at a small church in Mansfield, Texas, as the youth pastor. I was nineteen years old, full of zeal for what God had been doing in my life, and even more excited to impart it into the lives of the younger generation. The moment I stepped into ministry I began to deal with all sorts of insecure thoughts which resulted in me comparing myself to others, and putting my trust in what I could do versus what God could do. This chapter is inspired by Steven Furtick's book, *Crash the Chatterbox*. The chatterbox is where all the different voices are vying to overpower God's voice. Learning how to hear God's voice over yours, the devil's, and anything else that may put you on the wrong path takes time. The number one tool in the enemy's toolbox is deception. The Bible even goes as far in John 8:44 as describing Satan as, "The father of lies". That is a very strong statement that must be taken seriously concerning the spiritual warfare happening around our lives. We cannot be ignorant and think we are not a target for Satan. It was deception that took down Adam and Eve, and it is deception taking us down today.

By identifying the lies the enemy attempts to use against us, we will have a stronger defense during spiritual attacks. Think of the bad thoughts that are triggered when a situation occurs, or when you are having a bad day. What are your greatest insecurities? What causes you to shrink up due to fear?

Marriage is going to open up a whole new can of worms in regards to the thoughts going on your head. By learning how to deal with the chatter going on in your mind you will become even more emotionally stable, able to love unconditionally when your flesh desires to do otherwise.

Joyce Meyers explains the necessity for thinking rightly so well in her book, *The Battlefield of the Mind*. She states, "For the believer, right thinking is a vital necessity. A vital necessity is something that is so important that one simply cannot live without it—like a heartbeat is vital, or blood pressure is vital. These are things without which there is no life."[2]

The Voice of God vs. The Voice of Satan

The first step in learning to discern the difference between God's voice and Satan's voice is to embrace the fact that it is not an overnight process. It is the desire of every believer to hear God's voice above all others. A baby, as they are developing, will learn the voice of their parents only because

---

[2] Joyce Meyers, *The Battlefield of the Mind*, (New York: Faith Words), Chapter 2, (eBook version)

they hear it more often than anyone else's. If you have gone years with different thoughts running across your mind, but never taking the time to identify who was talking to you, then it will take a while to master the war within. The next step is to become a lover of God's Word, not by speech but by action.

God's Voice = Comfort, encouragement, conviction, direction.

Here are a list of biblical ways God will use to speak to you.

- **The Bible**: "All scripture is given by inspiration of God, and is profitable for doctrine, for reproof, for correction, for instruction in righteousness, that the man of God may be [complete], thoroughly equipped for every good work"(2 Timothy 3:16-17, KJ21)
- **The Holy Spirit**: "When the Spirit of Truth comes, He will guide you into all truth. He will not speak on His own but will tell you what He has heard. He will tell you about the future. He will bring me glory by telling you whatever he receives from me. (John 16:13-14, NLT)
- **The Prophetic**: (word of knowledge, word of wisdom, personal prophecy) "So, dear brothers and sisters, be eager to prophesy, and don't forbid speaking in tongues. But before that everything is done properly and in order (1 Corinthians 14:39-40, NLT)
- **Godly Leaders**: "Where no counsel is, the people fall: but in the multitude of counselors there is safety"(Proverbs 11:14, KJV)

- **Confirmation**: "By the mouth of two or three witnesses every fact may be confirmed" (Matthew 18:16, NASB)
- **The Presence of God**: "Let the peace of Christ rule in your hearts, to which indeed you were called in one body and be thankful (Colossians 3:15, ESV)
- **Life**: "And they have conquered him by the blood of the Lamb and by the word of their testimony, for they loved not their lives even unto death." (Revelation 12:11, ESV)

Satan's Voice

- **Condemnation**: So now there is no condemnation for those who belong to Christ Jesus. And because you belong to Him, the power of the life-giving Spirit has freed you from the power of sin that leads to death. (Romans 8:1, NLT)
- **Confusion**: For God is not a God of disorder but of peace. (1 Corinthians 14:33, NLT)
- **Challenges God's Truth**: The serpent was the shrewdest of all the wild animals the Lord God had made. One day he asked the woman, "Did God really say you must not eat the fruit from any of the trees in the garden?" (Genesis 3:1, NLT)
- **Tempts You**: Then the devil took him to the holy city, Jerusalem, to the highest point of the temple, and said, "If you are the Son of God, jump off!" (Matthew 4:5, NLT)

Chapter 18

Spiritual Gift / Character Check

Spiritual gifts are exactly that, gifts that are spiritual in nature. God gives each of His children gifts to be used for the benefit of advancing His Kingdom. Yes, you have a gift! It is so wonderful to be entrusted with something of such value. It can become a tragedy when you are given something that you either do not know you have or how to properly use what you have been given. Everyone has a minimum of one spiritual gift. There are many tools on line that can help you identify your spiritual gift or you can head over to 1 Corinthians 12 which is where the gifts are identified. There are more than sixteen spiritual gifts ranging from:

1. Leadership
2. Administration
3. Teaching
4. Word of Knowledge
5. Prophecy
6. Discernment
7. Exhortation
8. Shepherding
9. Faith

10. Evangelism
11. Apostleship
12. Service/helps
13. Mercy
14. Giving
15. Hospitality
16. Wisdom

Fruit of the Spirit Check

Marriage is going to require you to constantly live in the Spirit due to the extreme demand your spouse will make on your character and reactions. If you are operating in your flesh, you are not operating in the Spirit. You will save yourself from a lot of arguments and fights by yielding to this truth. Iron sharpening iron requires there to be a rubbing of two things together. That rub is not comfortable, but when seen with the proper perspective it can be a sign there is still growth to be accomplished. Blaming your spouse is the first thing many want to do when a situation occurs, but by applying this principle you will see all conflict is an opportunity for growth. Paul says in Galatians 5:16, "But I say, walk by the Sprit, and you will not gratify the desires of the flesh" (ESV). The only way to move closer to the fruit of the Spirit becoming more evident is to live and walk in the Spirit. What we do by the power of God's Spirit is seen as fruit, but what we do in the flesh is considered works. I have found it very powerful to pray these during my quiet times with God. I meditate upon each of them asking God to help me walk in the Spirit each day. These are the fruit of the Spirit outlined by Paul.

1. Love.
2. Joy.
3. Peace.
4. Patience.
5. Kindness.
6. Goodness.
7. Faithfulness.
8. Gentleness.
9. Self-control.

Chapter 19

Identify Your Negotiable and Non-Negotiable Qualities In Your Future Mate

In our society, we like to reject the thought of being able to fall in love with just one look simply because, reasonably it is not realistic I could easily tell you many stories of people who fell in love with just one look, but also many whose love was cultivated over time through friendship. In Song of Solomon 4:9 we enter into the middle of a romantic moment of two lovebirds, "You have ravished my heart, my treasure, my bride. I am overcome by one glance of your eyes, by a single bead of your necklace." I want to extend this thought, how was he able to have his heart stolen by her with one glance? In the book, *Dating with Pure Passion*, by Rob Eagar he states, "God created each of us as individuals with different likes and dislikes according to our personality and DNA." He then goes on to state, "One way to assist in the dating process is to know what you like." This is a great thought because many young adults DO NOT know what they like, or better put what they WANT in a future spouse (inside & out).

I believe this is one of the answers to how the lover guy was able to fall in love with the beloved girl with one glance of her eyes, because he saw her, and what he saw he had been waiting for(inside & out). I was not a believer of making a list but, after having a conversation with my Pastor one night when He asked me if I knew what my deal breakers were I wrote mine out. How would I recognize a counterfeit if she came? Well, many counterfeits came into my life over the course of my single years, and I can say it was having a list of the non-negotiable things that helped me say no when they poked their head up.

Non-Negotiable Qualities

The non-negotiable qualities include all the things you are confident that your future spouse must have. These qualities should be deal breakers. Here are a few examples, but note your non-negotiables will vary from someone else's. I will give you the list I had before I met my wife. This is straight from my journal written on December 25th, 2012.

1. A woman who loves Jesus more than me and is infatuated with worshipping and knowing God.
2. A woman who loves people and counts it an honor to be called to serve others by laying her life down for them in full time ministry.
3. A woman who desires to be a wife and a mother with a heart to serve her family.
4. A woman who is beautiful to me in every way, physically and emotionally.

Negotiable Qualities

The negotiable qualities are those that you desire for your spouse to have, but would not turn them away if they did not have them. Here were a few of mine.

1. A woman who could sing.
2. A woman with a passion for fashion.
3. A woman who loves kids.
4. A woman who has long hair.

Take some time to make your list. Remember be realistic, but also do not settle. When I met Natasha, she had everything on my non-negotiable list, but definitely missed a few on my negotiable list.

Chapter 20

Learn the Opposite Sex

I am an advocate for Godly friendships with the opposite sex, but I have also heard many arguments suggesting that Christian males and females cannot be friends. The majority of relationships are developed from friendship, which shows the reason why they are necessary, not only for potentially meeting your spouse, but also for learning how to have friendships that require boundaries. Yes, personal boundaries must be established. The key word there is "personal" which means you do not have to have a "talk" with your guy/girlfriend stating that you need to have boundaries. This can then communicate the wrong message possibly resulting in an awkward relationship.

View them like you would a brother or sister

The bible states in, 1 Timothy 5:1-2, "Do not rebuke an older man but encourage him as you would a father, younger men as brothers, older women as mothers, your younger women as sisters, in all purity" (ESV). Now, being real, you would not go to bed with your brother or sister, nor would you disrespect their boundaries. We do not need to get technical with the friendship turning into something more. The point is to treat them like you would a brother or sister. I still in many aspects treat my wife the way I would treat my sister, which is with respect, integrity, and honor. I have many opposite sex friendships that transitioned smoothly when I got married because they were healthy friendships where my wife was 100% included in them.

Don't automatically assess if they are "the one"

This happens all the time when you are in a group and there is that good looking person you've seen at church a couple of times, but now you're hanging out. Do not build a friendship with the motivation to find out if they are a potential. You will then begin to alter how you act around them and that robs the friendship of its purpose. Take it one day at a time!

Keep it Christ centered

When the friendship is Christ centered then lust, seduction, or any other perverted spirit cannot enter into it. This goes for both opposite and same sex friendships. Friends with benefits is a concept the world has taken on to stay away from commitment. This should not be for those representing Christ for we are the aroma of Christ to God among those who are being saved and among those who are perishing, according to 2 Corinthians 2:15 (ESV).

Section V

Chapter 21

Marriage Intelligence

I attended my first marriage conference my junior year of high school. It was being held at my church so I knew I could sneak in without anyone saying anything to me. It turned out that the only way for me to attend was by signing up to serve on the technical team. From there I began to read books on marriage further sparking my desire to marry God's way. Reading marriage books when you are unmarried helps give you a better understanding of marriage. You should have balance with this because no matter how much you know about marriage, no book will make you an expert. Desiring to do something that you know nothing about is a set up for failure. I can attest now being married that no matter how much you know about marriage, there is still much to learn. The same is true with anything you set out to become an expert in. You will not be able to control your future spouse, but by attaining biblical teaching on marriage you will be able to understand your future spouse. You will also be able to weather each storm you will face during your momentary marriage. As we begin to dive into marriage intelligence, it would be great for you to now grasp how your future marriage on earth is in actuality momentary. John Piper states in *Momentary Marriage,*

"So it is with marriage. It is a momentary gift. It may last a lifetime, or it may be snatched away on the honeymoon. Either way, it is short. Very soon the shadow will give way to Reality. The partial will pass into the Perfect. The troubled path will end in Paradise. And this momentary marriage will be swallowed up by Life. Christ will be all and in all. And the purpose of marriage will be complete. "

There is no marriage in heaven which gives us a glimpse of why God created it for here on Earth. In heaven all things will be fulfilled, and we will be with Christ. On Earth marriage is the grand opportunity to join in God's master plan to display the covenant love of Christ to His bride, the church.

Shaunti Feldhahn states in her book, *The Good News About Marriage*, that because the good news truth is that, in most cases, marriage is the most amazing, delightful, and profound earthly relationship any of us will ever know. The truth is that although most couples have to work at marriage, some will go through very hard times, most come out on the other side and enjoy each other for a lifetime. The truth is that although we can never look to marriage to make us happy, we need to be trumpeting the fact that when a couple chooses wisely and then takes the scary, but wonderful step of commitment for life, they are much more likely to have that abundant relationship they are hoping for." Is that not amazing! Nothing in your life that is most valuable to you came easy whether it was your education, career, or healthy relationships. Each of them required a lot of dedication and determination to make it to the place where you can say, "Wow, I'm so glad I didn't quit." That is marriage.

Why did God create marriage?

Gary Thomas, the author of *Sacred Marriage*, explains in his book, "God did not create marriage just to give us a pleasant means of repopulating the world and providing a steady societal institution to raise children. He planted marriage among humans as yet another signpost pointing to His own eternal, spiritual existence." Everything we do is first for the glory of God. He then goes on to say, "How can we use the challenges, joys, struggles and celebrations of marriage to draw close to God? What if God designed marriage to make us both happy and holy? Here is what the bible says about God's purpose of marriage.

Companionship: "Then the Lord God said, "It is not good for the man to be alone. I will make a helper who is just right for him." (Genesis 2:18, NLT)

Godly Children: "Didn't the Lord make you one with your wife? In body and spirit you are his. And what does he want? Godly children from your union. So guard your heart; remain loyal to your wife of your youth." (Malachi 2:15, NLT)

Reflect and Glorify God: "As the scriptures say, 'A man leaves his Father and Mother and is joined to his wife, and the two are united into one.' This is a great mystery, but it is an illustration of the way Christ and the church are one." (Ephesians 5:31-32, NLT)

John piper states, "The most ultimate thing we can say about marriage is that it exists for God's glory. That is, it exists to display God. Now [after looking at the passage in Ephesians] we can see how: Marriage is patterned after Christ's covenant relationship to the church. And therefore the highest meaning and most ultimate purpose of marriage is to put the covenant relationship of Christ and his church on display. That is why marriage exists.

Sexual Fulfillment: "The husband should fulfill his wife's sexual needs, and the wife should fulfill her husband's needs. The wife gives authority over her body to her husband, and the husband gives authority over his body to his wife." (1 Corinthians 7:3-4, NLT)

Sanctification: "For husbands, this means love your wives, just as Christ loved the church. He gave up his life for her to make her holy and clean, washed by the cleansing of God's word. He did this to present her to himself as a glorious church without a spot for wrinkle or any other blemish. Instead, she will be holy and without fault. (Ephesians 5:25-27, NLT)

"For wives, this means submit to your husbands as to the Lord. For a husband is the head of his wife as Christ is the head of the church. He is the Savior of his body, the church. As the church submits to Christ, so you wives should submit to your husbands in everything." (Ephesians 5:22-24, NLT)

Reb Bradley breaks it down so well by saying, "God's primary intention for marriage, is not what most of us imagine it to be. He has not designed marriage as a place where we can finally try to get our needs met [through a functional purpose or fashioned marriage merely as an illustration]. He has created it as something much better –something far grander than that. God intends to use marriage to accomplish a very important goal – one that is His *primary* goal for all Christians. *God's primary purpose for marriage is to use it to help shape us into the image of His Son.*

Compatibility versus Suitability

The first account of marriage in the bible is found with Adam and Eve in Genesis 3. God determined it was not good for man to be alone, so He created a woman who was suitable for him. Now, in today's culture we have become much more accustomed to compatibility versus suitability. Let's compare the two.

Compatible: able to exist or occur together without conflict.

Suitable: right or appropriate for a particular person, purpose, or situation.

Do you see why our generation has settled for a compatible person versus a suitable person? It is with a compatible person you focus more on external similarities such as: hobbies, friends, and interests.

But, just because you both can laugh together over a movie and play basketball against one another does not make them a suitable spouse for you.

Suitability is the biblical term used in Genesis to describe the type of mate God created for Adam. A person who is suitable for you goes beyond similar interests, but more into the purpose of God for that person's life. I agreed to not be in any relationship until after I graduated high school, which I successfully completed. I did not enter into my first committed relationship until my second year of college. She was a great girl who loved God, and had a true desire for ministry. Everything made sense in my mind because we were very compatible and all of my friends were in complete support of it. It started out as a friendship, and eventually developed into more.

I would spend hours with God begging Him to tell me if she was the one. I began to ride on the rollercoaster of emotions rather than being patient to get a peace from God. My emotions when I was on a high moment, resulted in me asking her into a committed relationship. From the first day I knew I had made a mistake. Because I did not want to look bad in front of my friends, and also hurt her, I continued in the relationship believing I would eventually fall for her. That relationship lasted six months which it was a constant up and down roller-coaster for me going back and forth whether she was my wife or not. One day I had a talk with a friend of mine that had been in a similar situation in a previous relationship. He said to me, "Jamal, God is too good to give you something you don't desire." I took that phrase to God, and asked Him, if it was true. For the first time in those six months I was honest with myself about how I really felt. I ended the relationship and fortunately we stayed pure during our time together. There had been no physical tie, but an emotional tie did develop because of the seriousness of the relationship. She was a great friend and we were very much compatible, but we were not suitable. When a person suits your life there will be a peace because it means God has blessed the now, and the later. The freedom that came over me after I ended the relationship was unexplainable in words. I knew I had put my life back into God hands, and I did not want to make the mistake of depending on myself ever again.

This is why it is imperative for you, as a believer, to pursue someone who is not only a believer, but also as spiritually mature as you. To determine suitability you must have the involvement of God in the relationship. A person who is suitable for you will be beneficial and necessary for God's plan for your life.

Spend time with a married couple that you want your marriage to be like

There were and still are so many married couples that I emulate. These couples allowed me to get a glimpse into what real marriage looks like. It was in the small things that I was able to learn the most important. It is the small things that make a marriage great. While in college, I got to serve the Director of the Institute, who was a jack-of-all-trades in regards to life and ministry. One key thing I learned from Adam McCain was each time we were meeting and his wife would call, he would stop what we were doing to take the call. He would then say to me, "Jamal, when you get married, your wife is priority over every and anything." I carried that nugget of truth into my marriage, and now no matter what I am doing, each time Natasha calls, I pick up.

Examine the good and bad of your parent's marriage

Your parents' marriage or lack thereof will have the greatest impact upon your marriage. What you grow up around inevitability you will recreate in your life. My parents did not have the most thriving marriage, so my mom would take time to help me see things from a woman's perspective, so I would know how to treat my future wife. That was the beginning point of me restructuring my learned behavior. My Spiritual Father, Matthew Stevenson, spent the majority of our pre-marital counseling walking through the ins and outs of our parent's marriage. He did that in order for us to be prepared for those same issues our parents faced if they arose in our marriage. By being prepared, it took the blame off of us and gave us grace to respond with understanding. After getting married we knew that our parent's marriage would have a major role, but it is not until you get into that first real misunderstanding that it becomes real.

Chapter 22

Keep Your Life Organized

Clean up what you mess up!

Your future spouse is not your parent, nor will they be your maid. Keeping your life organized takes teamwork. If you are messy before you marry then you can guarantee you will be messy after you marry. My wife and I come from two different upbringings. My parents are extra neat to the point that I have never in my history of knowing them seen their room less than perfect. So, growing up that standard was impressed upon me. I can hear my dad in my head right now, "Jamal, no woman likes a dirty man". Ha-ha!

Learn to love time management

One of the biggest adjustments to marriage is transitioning from managing your own time to now managing your time with someone else. There is no way out of it so you must learn now to love time management. I have seen this become a major problem in those just starting out in marriage because they want to keep doing things the way they used to without consulting their spouse is not going to work. Your spouse should know every place you are, not out of control, but out of respect. My wife texts me each time she arrives at a new destination, and I do the same for her.

One of my biggest issues was my work life. Being a bi-vocational Pastor requires me to do the majority of my church work on the go or at home. We need to have an organized day with a full schedule from the time we wake up to bed time in order to keep "everybody" happy. Everybody = my wife. Time management simply takes you spending twenty minutes on a Sunday evening to map out your week. Not only will those twenty minutes organize your week, but also help you do what matters most in life.

Chapter 23

Deal With Your Past

We all have a past and before you get married being transparent about it will bring healing that feels so much better than holding on to it. I thank God I was able to grab ahold of Christ at a young age because He guided me away from making decisions that would have affected my future. But, even though I was a lover of Christ, I still did things not up to His standard. It does not matter how much or how little you have done, being honest about what you have gone through is more about giving God glory than it is about you. The enemy wants to shut your mouth with shame, which is exactly what God desires to use to shame the devil! Unhealthy friendships with the opposite sex was a major part of my past. This was something I had to deal with before I got married. Even though they did not turn sexual, I would develop emotional ties which I consider just as destructive. I can be transparent about this now because I have shined the light on every part of my past so God may be glorified. It is not who I am that determines where I am going. I have been set free by the love and mercy of Jesus Christ.

If you have lived more than thirteen years on this planet then you have witnessed and experienced enough to need a tune up. When you purchase a new car the first thing you do is drive off excited that you are sporting a brand new vehicle. I remember when I got my first truck at the age of sixteen. I had worked two jobs in order to save up the money to get it. When I made it home after cruising around town in it, I got out and just stared at it in awe. Then, my dad comes out of the house and says, "Now, how you take care of it will determine how long you have it. Give me your keys until you have read the entire owner's manual." I looked at him like he was joking, which he was not at all. Who does that? I reached into the glove compartment and opened up the manual, and while reading it, there was a section called, maintenance schedule. It had for every mileage milestone what maintenance you should have done for the vehicle in order for you the car to perform at its highest. This is the same for us when we become new believers. We need maintenance.

When you become a new creation in Christ, your spirit is regenerated, but your mind is not. Your mind must be renewed. You still can think back to those sinful decisions you made, or the type of people you surrounded yourself around. My pastor teaches, "No sin is committed without the influence of Satan." We can see examples of this in two major temptations in the bible, the first being Adam and Eve, and the second being Jesus in the wilderness. In both accounts we find Satan attempting to deceive them with trickery and lies. Now being in Christ you need to renew your mind, purify your heart, and set yourself anew.

Get Down to the Root

Getting down to the root of my issues was not an overnight thing. The first step is discovering the root, then getting rid of it by faith in the power of God's redeeming grace! This is done through the inner healing and deliverance the Holy Spirit brings to souls. Deliverance is simply the process by which you come out of agreement with various evil spirits that have been given access to your life through generational curses or your own sinful actions. Joyce Meyers says, "Is there something in your past or your present that is causing problems with your emotions or thoughts? If we were honest, all of us would admit there are times when we struggle with wrong thoughts and the unhealthy emotions they create. Sometimes this can even lead to depression or other serious ongoing conditions that keep us from being emotionally and mentally whole."–*Battlefield of the Mind*. God desires to make you whole by dealing with the root of your actions and past experiences. Becoming whole requires coming to God with all of you, including your feelings and thoughts.

> He heals the brokenhearted and binds up their wounds [curing their pains and their sorrows]. (Psalm 147:3, ESV, brackets not in original)

Make Room for the New

We find in the book of Isaiah 43:19, "*God says, 'For I am about to do something **new**. See, I have already begun! Do you not see it?'* This scripture was given to me prophetically at the beginning of July, which was my one year mark since moving to Chicago. That scripture along with some powerful insight regarding this next year of my life got me REALLY excited. My mind began to roam regarding what "new thing" God was about to do in my life. While happy and expectant, **I was unaware of the requirements this word came with.**

While reading over Isaiah 43, God spoke to me saying, *"You desire for me to bring the new, but you must first get rid of the old."* **Jesus does not personally destroy areas of our lives that are blocking Him out, but points them out and tells us to destroy them.** Desiring all God has for you is just the beginning and it must be followed up with making room for Him in your life. It is the small foxes that spoil the vine, and in your life there are small things that could be preventing Him from showing up. There could be a range of things from unhealthy relationships to selfish character that stems to destructive environments. God prunes us in so that we be more fruitful for Him. We must learn to embrace this time of cleansing, for it is Him saying to you: "You make room, and I'll bring in the new".

History with your Family

Your relationship with your family will play a major role in your marriage. God makes a promise in the Ten Commandments for those who honor their Father and Mother, that they will live a long life. No family is the same, we all have witnessed things done by our families that we are not proud of, and at the same token, things we thank God for. My parents were the most hardworking, loving, and generous people I know, to which I am beyond thankful for. I did not have a perfect childhood, but I learned to honor them no matter what. How you love your family through challenging situations will reflect how you will love your spouse. I remember growing up and I compared my family to other families, and that resulted in me looking down on them. God had to teach me to see them the way He sees all of His children. We are all a work in progress. Wherever you are with your family whether it be your mom, dad, siblings, or close relative, make every effort to love, honor, and appreciate them for who they are. It was so important to me that my wife had a healthy relationship with her family because I knew it would play a major role in our marriage. Your future spouse will inherit your family, so prepare now for them to inherit something you have done everything to love.

Chapter 24

Live Above Reproach

I was driving with one of my good friends, Jeremy, from my home in Monroe, Louisiana, headed to Dallas, Texas, to catch a flight back to Chicago. It was the middle of the night, and my friend was asleep. Music is blasting to keep me awake, while my friend snores away. I look into the distance and notice up ahead on the highway there were headlights headed in our direction. I wake Jeremy up saying, "Man, is that car headed in our direction?" He yells, "Bro, are we going the wrong way"? I double check to make sure we are on the right side of the highway. The car is still coming right at us with no intention of moving over, so I quickly pull the car over into the median, and a few seconds later the car, now truck, flew past us at full speed. My leg was shaking out of complete shock of what had just happened. I called the cops right away to notify them. They were already aware and had sent a cop car to handle it.

What was so significant about this story is how our first thought, due to how confident the other driver was coming at us, was to second guess if we were on the right side of the road. This is the same thing that happens when you are living your life above reproach. Because many are not doing it, it is easy to question if you are living right when someone else is living a life of what appears to be free fun doing whatever they desire to do. This is why living above reproach is not popular, because when the majority are going in the wrong direction, you have to be strong enough to continue heading in the right direction. When you go to the hospital the majority in there are sick, but that does not make sickness normal. Choosing purity, no sex before marriage, righteous relationships, and marriage God's way will not be easy, but it will be worth it!

As you prepare yourself for the biggest decision besides saying "yes" to Christ, your main agenda is to get yourself right. In the midst of doing that we can lose sight that we are still human which means you will make mistakes, you will miss the bull's eyes, and you will fall down. When this does occur, be honest about it. Do not masquerade like things are perfect in order to impress the person you are interested in. This is why I am a proponent of observing a person in their world before you take a serious interest in someone. God knew what he was doing when he set it up for me and Natasha to meet through Facebook. I was limited to how much I could observe her other than stalk her pictures. Crazy. A little. It worked. When we did begin to get to know one another, you automatically share all of the wonderful things you have done, and everything God is doing. It was not until a week before Natasha was scheduled to come out to Chicago for us to meet face-to-face that we had a very honest conversation. I communicated some of my fears and concerns, and she communicated hers. The ability to be honest did not start here, but started well before we even met one another. The Bible states in1 Timothy 1:19, "Cling to your faith in Christ, and keep your conscience clear. For some have deliberately disobeyed their consciences and their faith has been shipwrecked." Keeping your conscience clear requires you being honest about issues, challenges, and sinful actions you have done. Becoming great at doing this now, before marriage, will make it a piece of cake within marriage because you will not build your life around all your highlight moments.

Commit to Purity

You can guarantee that if you abstain from having sexual contact, whether physical or emotional during your waiting season, the value you place upon yourself and your future spouse will last the entirety of your marriage. This value adds volumes to your sex life in marriage. Studies show that those who wait to have sex are happier in the long run. I do not look at my wife like a piece of meat, but a treasure worthy of being handled with tender care. I proved that to her by denying my flesh, and leading the stand for our purity. Our wedding night was the most beautiful encounter as we exchanged our gifts to another. Our marriage was established on a sure foundation with God in the center of it all. Married people have the best sex! Even if you have already had sex before the reading of this book, please note the power of God's forgiveness. Refresh that commitment now to God to preserve your body for your spouse.

Chapter 25

Die to I

The most memorable moment of my life was underway. It is my wedding day, and everyone who has played a major role in my life and my wife's life were sitting before us. The music begins to play and she proceeds down the aisle with her father. Now, most men are staring at their bride some, even crying. I actually had a flash back to the life changing experience I had with God eight years before.

This experience was that I almost gave away something very precious to me to someone who did not deserve it. God encountered me in that moment saying, "Jamal if you compromise now you will compromise for the rest of your life, and trust me I have something so much better for you." I halted everything, kicked the girl out of my room, got on my face declaring to God I would no longer serve Him half-hearted, but I was going all in. That was the day, I died. The flashback felt like a quick second, but when I came back to reality, my bride had made it down the aisle. I now had tears in my eyes as God's words spoken to me eight years before were being fulfilled. I stood hand-in-hand with my bride, both being virgins, ready to commit our lives to one another.

Galatians 2:20, which is one of my life verses, states, "For I have been crucified with Christ, it is no longer I who lives, but Christ who lives in me, and the life I now live, I live by faith in the Son of God who loves me, and gave Himself for me" (ESV).

Your future marriage will require you to have a biblical perspective of your life. Dying to yourself and picking up your cross daily is the number one prerequisite for living a life hidden in Christ. In a day and time where the humanistic agenda is on the rise we must be on guard. Humanism is the stance that emphasizes the value of human beings over anything else. Well, the anything else includes God. There is nothing wrong with being valued, but when we value ourselves to the point that it eradicates our need for God, then we have a problem.

It will take much discipline and the consistent application of God's word to live this lifestyle, but once you tap into the joy of it, you will understand why it all becomes worth it. Your love story does not begin when you meet your spouse, it began the day you said, "I will prepare myself for the union that will last a lifetime."

My Prayer over you

> *Father, I thank you for the faithfulness you have shown to even lead your son/daughter to read this book. I ask, by your divine will, that you will continue to guide them on this path towards Christ-likeness that they may be fully prepared for their suitable mate. May they not grow anxious in well doing, but declare your goodness each day.*

Guard their hearts and minds as they walk this life out by faith and not by sight. And, I declare over their future spouse now that they will find one another in your perfect timing.

In Jesus Name, Amen!

Hallelujah.

40647533R00078

Made in the USA
San Bernardino, CA
25 October 2016